PRAYER JOURNAL FOR GROWTH

Growing in Your Relationship with God

SUSAN A. LUND

WESTBOW
PRESS®
A DIVISION OF THOMAS NELSON
& ZONDERVAN

WestBow Press books may be ordered through booksellers or by contacting:

WestBow Press
A Division of Thomas Nelson & Zondervan
1663 Liberty Drive
Bloomington, IN 47403
www.westbowpress.com
844-714-3454

ISBN: 978-1-6642-9336-6 (sc)
ISBN: 978-1-6642-9338-0 (hc)
ISBN: 978-1-6642-9337-3 (e)

Print information available on the last page.

WestBow Press rev. date: 03/01/2023

Dedication

This convenient, easy-to-use prayer journal is dedicated to you the reader and writer. As you journal your prayers, may you experience personal and spiritual growth along with the inward joy that comes from knowing and trusting God each and every day.

My Story

One year prior to finding out my mom had cancer, God led me to journal my prayers. Prior to that time, the thought had never occurred to me. During one of the most challenging years of my life, God strengthened me and comforted me as I prayed and journaled my prayers.

I am in awe of how God knows our every need. I believe God drew me close to strengthen me, comfort me, and ultimately lead my mom to accept Jesus Christ as her personal Savior, just two weeks before she passed away and went home to be with the Lord. This was one of many demonstrations of God's love for my mom and me. We serve such a great God.

I published my initial prayer journal out of gratitude for how God had blessed me with the intent to bless and help others grow in their relationships with God. I began teaching courses at church and used my journal as a complement to small groups. People loved learning how to journal their prayers and strengthen their prayer life, growing their relationships with God.

The problem was that I was thinking too small. I published it for women and learned they wanted one for the men in their lives: their fathers, grandfathers, husbands, children, brothers, and friends. That experience, learning, and the leadership of God in my life led me to publish this prayer journal. As a result, it is for everyone who wants to grow in their relationships with God. Just like God led me, as you grow in your relationship with God, He will lead you too!

This is a simple, easy-to-use prayer journal that will help you grow in your relationship with God. Writing out your prayers helps you hear the voice of God, feel the presence of God, and experience the greatness of God daily. As you journal your prayers, may you experience personal and spiritual growth along with the inward joy that comes from knowing and trusting God more every day.

Congratulations!

You have taken the first step toward strengthening the most important relationship in your lifetime—the only relationship that you will have for a lifetime—your relationship with God.

This prayer journal is a convenient, easy-to-use guide for personal growth and practical application. It is designed to help you enrich your faith and embrace the awesome glory of God. Simply devote ten minutes each day to journaling your daily walk with God. In doing so, you will experience tremendous rewards and lasting blessings.

Journaling helps you

- develop the spiritual discipline required to grow in your relationship with God;
- create spiritual vitality—recognizing God's presence in your daily life, staying in constant contact with God, seeking His guidance and direction in your daily life, and observing how God's plan for your life unfolds;
- hear the voice of God and experience the presence of God;
- experience the inward joy of knowing and trusting God in all situations;
- express gratitude and count your blessings;
- confess your sins and seek forgiveness;
- write out prayer requests for your loved ones and those in need;
- glorify God in all you say and do;
- ask him to use you as an instrument to glorify Him; and
- make a difference in the lives of others!

Who Can Benefit from Journaling?

Anyone who wants to grow in their relationship with God can benefit from journaling. Leaders, mothers, fathers, grandparents, daughters, sons, sisters, brothers, friends, coworkers, neighbors, traveling professionals—anyone who is willing to commit just ten minutes a day to prayer and the growth of the most important relationship they will ever have, their relationship with God. Recognize God's awesome power and presence! There are no limits to its applications.

Personal use. Journal for your own personal growth and practical application.

Bible study groups. Journal in conjunction with your study guide to reflect on how God is working in your daily life and how you are responding to His guidance. Journal collectively within the study group. Journal for one week, and then pass it on to every group member. When journaling is complete, return the journal to the group leader, and discuss the ways that God's presence has touched the lives of each participant.

Leadership teams. Strengthen your leadership team by journaling together.

How Can You Use This Journal?

This journal can be used to grow your relationship with God and as a compliment to your study, a small group, or an event. Journaling what you learn and how God works in your life and uses you to serve others as well as living a life that honors God helps you grow and experience the greatness of our God.

Small group. Use this journal as a compliment to discuss your sermon and what you learned or a Bible study.

Small group study—*Prayer Journaling for Growth.* Use this journal as an independent study to walk through and share journaling your prayers, or invite Susan to speak to your small group.

Women's retreats. Include in program and course materials.

Junior high and senior high school retreats. Include in the program and materials.

Young adult groups. The Bible says that every generation must choose to serve God. Young adults love this simple, easy-to-use tool. Invite Susan to speak. Susan loves to inspire, equip, and empower the next generation!

Mother's Day gift. Give your mom, grandma, or mother-in-law the gift of a prayer journal to help her grow in her relationship with God.

Father's Day gift. Give your dad, grandpa, or father-in-law the gift of a prayer journal to help him grow in his relationship with God.

Birthday gift. Give your friends, family members, and children a special gift that will help them grow the most important relationship they will ever have—their relationship with God.

Wedding gift. One of the most important things a woman or man can do is pray for their spouse and marriage. God will strengthen the marriages of those who pray for His leadership and to have a blessed marriage.

New believer gift. If you know anyone who has just become a Christian, this is a great tool to help them grow in their relationship with God.

Leadership teams. Pastors, CEOs, VPs, directors, and managers— when leaders grow their relationships with God, everyone benefits!

To engage Susan to speak, call 1 (800) 281-6084. All talks are customized to your needs.

Guidelines for Journaling

Monthly Goals, Review, and Reflection

Goals. As you set monthly spiritual goals, you may find it helpful to sit silently for ten minutes and ask God to reveal—in words and images—what He believes you need to work on during the next month. Observe how He speaks to you and how you hear Him.

Review and reflection. At the end of each month, review your journal entries, and reflect on God's guidance in your daily life. Take a red pen, and record how and when God answered your prayers. When you need a reminder of God's love, review past blessings. Then turn to the scriptures, and notice how unchanging His love is. As you reflect on your monthly goals and daily entries, answer the following questions:

- Are there key themes and patterns emerging?
- What are your prayer habits (frequency, posture, time of day, length, etc.)?
- Is there anything you want to improve upon?
- What obstacles prevented you from journaling daily, and how can you overcome them?
- How did God bless you this month?
- How did you glorify God this month?
- What did you learn from your prayers and the responses from God?
- What adjustments can you make in your life because of what you learned?
- How have you grown in your faith from journaling this month?

Daily Reflections

What can you do to grow in your relationship with God today? There are many ways to nourish yourself spiritually, such as reading the Bible, praying, listening to praise and worship music, journaling, and serving others. Every day, commit to activities that help you grow in your relationship with God.

What can you praise and thank God for today? Praise acknowledges God for who He is, and thanking God acknowledges God for all He has done. Praise, thanks, and prayer takes the focus off yourself and helps you connect with the heart of God. Praise and adoration of God proclaims His power and authority in our lives. It refocuses our communication with God on His will, His power, and His presence in our daily lives. Thanking God daily helps you remember God's goodness and love. Expect His favor on your life. When you do, you will find that your heart has elevated from daily distractions to lasting confidence and trust in God.

What sins did you commit? Every day, Satan tries to stop the work of God. He tries to distract you and shift your focus away from God. These distractions can include things like busyness, self-centeredness, jealousy, doubt, temptations, accusations, and greed. It is important to make prayer a priority—to ask God for help in defeating Satan, to exercise your authority as a believer, and to repent and ask God for forgiveness of sins.

Who needs your prayers? Prayer requests provide an opportunity to extend God's love and compassion, which focus on the needs of others. When you pray, be specific. Prayer requests can be categorized into four areas: personal, family and friends, community, and worldwide. God hears and answers every prayer. Observe how God blesses you and those you pray for.

What did you learn from journaling today? Journaling, praying, and reading the Bible enhance your awareness of God's presence and provide guidance in your daily life. Making a daily commitment to these activities helps you to become all God designed you to be and to reach your full potential. Talking and listening to God helps you know and love God more, and it increases your understanding of who God is and what His will for you is. Make note of these insights to remember God's faithfulness in your life.

What adjustments can you make as a result of what you learned today? A Christian life is a changed life. Listening is absorbing and accepting the information you read and hear about God. Learning is understanding its meaning and implications. Obeying is putting all you have learned and understood into action. All three parts are essential for a growing relationship with God. Invite God to transform your heart and to change you to become all He designed you to be.

Praying

Take time to write out your prayers daily. Set aside ten minutes every day. Begin your day by reading God's Word, praying, and journaling.

How to pray. Prayer is your personal conversation with God. Be open and honest with yourself and with God. He knows your heart's desires and your every need. He will guide you if you ask Him to. Focus on who you are praying to—our Father, who art in heaven.

Consistent communication is the foundation of all intimate relationships. The secret to a close relationship with God is to earnestly pray to Him every day and to listen to what He says. After all, prayer is a two-way communication: speaking to God and listening to God. Consistent communication is fundamental to any friendship and certainly necessary for an intimate relationship with God.

The Power of Prayer

[18]The Lord is near to all who call upon Him,
To all who call upon Him in truth.
(Psalm 145:18 NKJV)

[10]Be still, and know that I am God; I will be exalted among
the nations, I will be exalted in the earth!
(Psalm 46:10 NKJV)

[16]Rejoice always, [17]pray without ceasing, [18]in everything give
thanks; for this is the will of God in Christ Jesus for you.
(1 Thessalonians 5:16–18 NKJV)

[13]And whatever you ask in My name, that I will do, that the Father may
be glorified in the Son. [14]If you ask anything in My name, I will do it.
(John 14:13–14 NKJV)

[14]If My people who are called by My name will humble themselves, and
pray and seek My face, and turn from their wicked ways, then I will
hear from heaven, and will forgive their sin and heal their land.
(2 Chronicles 7:14 NKJV)

[15]Lord, I wait for you; you will answer, Lord my God.
(Psalm 38:15 NIV)

[35]Very early in the morning, while it was still dark, Jesus got up, left
the house and went off to a solitary place, where he prayed.
(Mark 1:35 NIV)

[6]Be anxious for nothing, but in everything by prayer and
supplication, with thanksgiving, let your requests be made known
to God; [7]and the peace of God, which surpasses all understanding,
will guard your hearts and minds through Christ Jesus.
(Philippians 4:6–7 NKJV)

[12]For the eyes of the Lord are on the righteous, And His ears are open to
their prayers; But the face of the Lord is against those who do evil.
(1 Peter 3:12 NKJV)

[9]The things which you learned and received and heard and saw
in me, these do, and the God of peace will be with you.
(Philippians 4:9 NKJV)

[9]If we confess our sins, He is faithful and just to forgive us *our* sins
and to cleanse us from all unrighteousness.
(1 John 1:9 NKJV)

"[11]For I know the plans I have for you," declares the Lord, "plans to prosper
you and not to harm you, plans to give you hope and a future."
(Jeremiah 29:11 NIV)

Setting Goals for Spiritual Growth

Without goals, it is easy to get distracted, lose focus, and get busy with activities that don't lead to productivity. Distraction is a trap from the enemy. God wants us to live a focused, productive life and to run our races with endurance. Goals help us to stay focused on things that matter most, like growing in our relationship with God. Goals also direct us and help us to live productive lives that honor God and to run our races with endurance. Living a productive life is being a good steward of everything God gives us. Goals help us plan and be intentional to steward the resources God gives us. These resources include our time, gifts, relationships, money, and opportunities to serve and fulfill the plans God has for us.

> Therefore we also, since we are surrounded by so great a cloud of witnesses, let us lay aside every weight, and the sin which so easily ensnares us, and let us run with endurance the race that is set before us, (Hebrews 12:1 NKJV)

I have set goals all my life. There was no way I would have grown so much in my relationship with God and discovered my purpose and His plan for my life if I hadn't sought God and set goals to grow in my relationship with Him. Goals help me to keep the main thing, the main thing—which for me, is my relationship with God. Goals help us to know and love Him more every day. Faith begins with action steps. Goals help us to take steps of faith to know, trust, and rely on God more. God is a plan-filled God, and blessed are those who plan. Proverbs 21:5 says, "The plans of the diligent lead surely to plenty, But those of everyone who is hasty, surely to poverty" (NKJV).

If you are new to goal setting, I want to encourage you to just start. I have created a sample to guide you. Successful goal setting includes creating SMART goals:

S—specific
M—measurable
A—attainable with God's help

R—relevant
T—time-bound

One way to get started is to pray.

Lord, reveal to me what You want me to work on this month to grow in my relationship with You. I want to know You more and love You more. Reveal to me steps that I can take to grow in my relationship with You. Help me make growing in my relationship with You a priority in my life. In Jesus's name, I pray, amen.

Sample

Spiritual Goals for the Month of
<u>April</u>

What are my three spiritual goals for this month?

1. Grow in my dependence on God by seeking His counsel first in all situations.
2. Join a small group this month.
3. Serve by leading a small group in prayer journaling to help others grow spiritually.

Why do I want to achieve these goals?

1. Because I know God has wisdom that I don't have. I recognize my need for His wisdom.
2. Seeking God's wisdom first helps me make better decisions and honor Him.
3. Self-reliance is prideful and hinders my relationship with God.
4. In the Bible, God tells us that we need fellowship with other believers to grow. He wants us to make this a priority. We grow when we are in a community with believers.
5. We are blessed to be a blessing to others. God knows that our greatest joy comes from blessing others with what He gives us and glorifying Him.

What obstacles do I anticipate?

Making time to grow spiritually and serve could be an obstacle.

How will I overcome these obstacles? What support do I need (prayer, scripture, Bible study, a spiritual director, a Christian friend, etc.)?

I will put it on my calendar to sign up for a small group at church this weekend. I will talk to my pastor next week, to find out what I need to do to lead a small group. I will pray and ask God to help me follow through with making Him a priority.

How will achieving these goals help me glorify God?

God wants us to depend on Him and seek Him first. When we are in fellowship with others and encourage others to grow, we grow in our relationship with Him, and that pleases God. It honors God when we grow in our relationship with other believers. God loves it when we serve others and glorify Him. God also rewards those who serve. Serving is an expression of our love for God and for others.

Spiritual Goals for the Month of

_____

What are my three spiritual goals for this month?

1.
2.
3.

Why do I want to achieve these goals?

1. _____
2. _____
3. _____
4. _____
5. _____

What obstacles do I anticipate?

_____
_____

How will I overcome these obstacles? What support do I need (prayer, scripture, Bible study, a spiritual director, a Christian friend, etc.)?

_____
_____
_____
_____
_____

How will achieving these goals help me glorify God?

_____
_____
_____
_____
_____

Sample Daily Reflections

Today is ___April 10, 2023___ S (M) T W TH F S

1. **What can I do to grow my relationship with God today?**
   - ☑ Read the Bible
   - ☑ Prayed alone
   - ☑ Prayed with a friend, family member, or spouse
   - ☑ Shared my faith
   - ☑ Listened to and/or sang to Christian music
   - ☑ Wrote in my prayer journal
   - ☑ Served others

2. **What can I praise and thank God for today?**
   Lord, I praise You and give thanks, for Your love endures forever. Lord, I praise You because You are in control and have overcome the world. Thank You for the discipline to read the Bible, spend time with You, and journal. Thank You for using me to serve a coworker by listening and encouraging her today. Thank You, Lord, for using me to share my faith with a friend.

3. **What sins did I commit?**
   Lord, reveal to me any sin, so I can repent. Forgive me, and keep me from deliberate wrongs.

4. **Who needs my prayers today?**
   Lord, I pray that You will bless every person who is reading this today. I pray for spiritual revival within every family member. Lord, transform their hearts so they desire to know You more. Lord, transform and align my heart's desires with Your purpose, Your Word, and Your Will. I want to know You more and love You more today. Lord, help me understand what You are doing in the world and how I can partner with You today. Help me bless others and glorify You today. Lord, guide me to provide encouragement for my family, build them up, pray for them, and speak life into them.

5. **What did I learn today?**
   Writing out my prayers helps me to focus my thoughts on you, Lord. Doing so increases my awareness of Your presence in my daily life.

6. **What adjustments can I make in my life because of what I learned today?**
   I can start and finish every day by reading the Bible and praying to ask God what He wants me to do. Lord, what do you want me to think, say, and do today? I want to make it a priority to do what You say to do.

Sample Prayers

As you write out your prayers, don't be concerned with how they sound but to whom you are praying—our Creator, almighty King, and heavenly Father along with the Holy Spirit, our Helper. Simply pray with an open heart. As you grow in your relationship with God, your prayer life will mature. Here are a few sample prayers:

Lord, thank You for this day. Thank You for Your leadership in my life. I praise You, for Your thoughts are higher than my thoughts. I want to know and love You more today. I pray that You watch over and guide me and my family today. Open our eyes and hearts to partner with You today, Lord. I pray that any of Satan's attempts to enter our thoughts, words, or actions be cast at the foot of the cross, covered with the blood of the lamb, and rendered powerless in the name of Jesus Christ. Fill our hearts with Your love, peace, wisdom, and will, Lord. Help us look to You throughout our busy days and seek Your wisdom. Help us find quiet time to listen to Your guidance and feel Your presence in every situation and every conversation. Direct our steps, and help us make God-honoring choices. Lord, use us as instruments to bless others and to glorify You in all that we think, say, and do today. In Jesus's name, I pray, amen.

Almighty King, three years prior to creating this initial journal, when You planted the seed within me to begin a prayer journal, little did I know You would use this as a tool to strengthen my relationship with You. Furthermore, I had no idea that this prayer journal would be used to encourage other people and their families to grow in their relationships with You. Lord, I praise You for knowing our every need and for Your unconditional love. Lord, I pray that every person who uses this journal may discover the inward joy of strengthening their relationship with You. Whether he or she is a baby Christian or a mature Christian, may each person become aware of Your constant love, presence, and guidance in their daily lives. May they become keenly aware of Your voice as You speak to them. Give them the spiritual discipline to journal daily and transform their hearts' desires to know you like never before, amen.

Search my heart, Lord, and reveal to me whatever I need to work on. Protect me from sin, and keep me from deliberate wrongs. Transform my heart to Your desires. Give me the discipline and desire to serve You with my whole heart. In Jesus's name, I pray, amen.

When the disciples asked Jesus how to pray, Jesus replied,

> This, then, is how you should pray:
> "Our Father in heaven, hallowed be your name, your kingdom come, your will be done, on earth as it is in heaven. Give us today our daily bread. And forgive us our debts, as we also have forgiven our debtors. And lead us not into temptation, but deliver us from the evil one. For if you forgive other people when they sin against you, your heavenly Father will also forgive you. But if you do not forgive others their sins, your Father will not forgive your sins." (Matthew 6:9–15 NIV)

Start your day putting on the full armor of God.

> [10]Finally, be strong in the Lord and in his mighty power. [11]Put on the full armor of God, so that you can take your stand against the devil's schemes.
> [12]For our struggle is not against flesh and blood, but against the rulers, against the authorities, against the powers of this dark world and against the spiritual forces of evil in the heavenly realms.
> [13]Therefore put on the full armor of God, so that when the day of evil comes, you may be able to stand your ground, and after you have done everything, to stand.
> [14]Stand firm then, with the belt of truth buckled around your waist, with the breastplate of righteousness in place, [15]and with your feet fitted with the readiness that comes from the gospel of peace.
> [16]In addition to all this, take up the shield of faith, with which you can extinguish all the flaming arrows of the evil one.
> [17]Take the helmet of salvation and the sword of the Spirit, which is the word of God. (Ephesians 6:10–17 NIV)

There is power in prayer. When we pray, things change for the better! God loves you and wants to bless you. Don't miss out on the opportunity to be a blessing to others and receive God's blessings today.

Spiritual Goals for the Month of

_____

What are my three spiritual goals for this month?

1.
2.
3.

Why do I want to achieve these goals?

1. _____
2. _____
3. _____
4. _____
5. _____

What obstacles do I anticipate?

_____
_____

How will I overcome these obstacles? What support do I need (prayer, scripture, Bible study, a spiritual director, a Christian friend, etc.)?

_____
_____
_____
_____
_____

How will achieving these goals help me glorify God?

_____
_____
_____
_____
_____

Today is _____ S M T W TH F S

1. **What can I do to grow my relationship with God today?**
    - ☐ Read the Bible
    - ☐ Pray alone
    - ☐ Pray with a friend, family member, or spouse
    - ☐ Share my faith
    - ☐ Listen to and/or sing to Christian music
    - ☐ Write in my prayer journal
    - ☐ Serve others

2. **What can I praise and thank God for today?**

    _____

    _____

    _____

    _____

    _____

3. **What sins did I commit?**

    _____

    _____

4. **Who needs my prayers?**

    _____

    _____

    _____

    _____

5. **What did I learn today?**

    _____

    _____

6. **What adjustments can I make in my life because of what I learned today?**

    _____

    _____

Prayers

Today is _____ S M T W TH F S

1. **What can I do to grow my relationship with God today?**
   - ☐ Read the Bible
   - ☐ Pray alone
   - ☐ Pray with a friend, family member, or spouse
   - ☐ Share my faith
   - ☐ Listen to and/or sing to Christian music
   - ☐ Write in my prayer journal
   - ☐ Serve others

2. **What can I praise and thank God for today?**

   _____
   _____
   _____
   _____
   _____

3. **What sins did I commit?**

   _____
   _____

4. **Who needs my prayers?**

   _____
   _____
   _____
   _____
   _____

5. **What did I learn today?**

   _____
   _____

6. **What adjustments can I make in my life because of what I learned today?**

   _____
   _____

Prayers

Today is _____ S M T W TH F S

1. **What can I do to grow my relationship with God today?**
   - ☐ Read the Bible
   - ☐ Pray alone
   - ☐ Pray with a friend, family member, or spouse
   - ☐ Share my faith
   - ☐ Listen to and/or sing to Christian music
   - ☐ Write in my prayer journal
   - ☐ Serve others

2. **What can I praise and thank God for today?**

   _____
   _____
   _____
   _____
   _____

3. **What sins did I commit?**

   _____
   _____

4. **Who needs my prayers?**

   _____
   _____
   _____
   _____

5. **What did I learn today?**

   _____
   _____

6. **What adjustments can I make in my life because of what I learned today?**

   _____
   _____

Prayers

Today is _____ S M T W TH F S

1. **What can I do to grow my relationship with God today?**

   ☐ Read the Bible

   ☐ Pray alone

   ☐ Pray with a friend, family member, or spouse

   ☐ Share my faith

   ☐ Listen to and/or sing to Christian music

   ☐ Write in my prayer journal

   ☐ Serve others

2. **What can I praise and thank God for today?**

   _____

   _____

   _____

   _____

   _____

3. **What sins did I commit?**

   _____

   _____

4. **Who needs my prayers?**

   _____

   _____

   _____

   _____

   _____

5. **What did I learn today?**

   _____

   _____

6. **What adjustments can I make in my life because of what I learned today?**

   _____

   _____

Prayers

Today is _____ S   M   T   W   TH   F   S

1. **What can I do to grow my relationship with God today?**
    ☐ Read the Bible
    ☐ Pray alone
    ☐ Pray with a friend, family member, or spouse
    ☐ Share my faith
    ☐ Listen to and/or sing to Christian music
    ☐ Write in my prayer journal
    ☐ Serve others

2. **What can I praise and thank God for today?**

    _____
    _____
    _____
    _____
    _____

3. **What sins did I commit?**

    _____
    _____

4. **Who needs my prayers?**

    _____
    _____
    _____
    _____
    _____

5. **What did I learn today?**

    _____
    _____

6. **What adjustments can I make in my life because of what I learned today?**

    _____
    _____

Prayers

Today is _____ S M T W TH F S

1. **What can I do to grow my relationship with God today?**
   - ☐ Read the Bible
   - ☐ Pray alone
   - ☐ Pray with a friend, family member, or spouse
   - ☐ Share my faith
   - ☐ Listen to and/or sing to Christian music
   - ☐ Write in my prayer journal
   - ☐ Serve others

2. **What can I praise and thank God for today?**

   _____
   _____
   _____
   _____
   _____

3. **What sins did I commit?**

   _____
   _____

4. **Who needs my prayers?**

   _____
   _____
   _____
   _____
   _____

5. **What did I learn today?**

   _____
   _____

6. **What adjustments can I make in my life because of what I learned today?**

   _____
   _____

Prayers

Today is _____ S M T W TH F S

1. **What can I do to grow my relationship with God today?**
   ☐ Read the Bible
   ☐ Pray alone
   ☐ Pray with a friend, family
      member, or spouse
   ☐ Share my faith
   ☐ Listen to and/or sing
      to Christian music
   ☐ Write in my prayer journal
   ☐ Serve others

2. **What can I praise and thank God for today?**

   _____
   _____
   _____
   _____
   _____

3. **What sins did I commit?**

   _____
   _____

4. **Who needs my prayers?**

   _____
   _____
   _____
   _____
   _____

5. **What did I learn today?**

   _____
   _____

6. **What adjustments can I make in my life because of what I learned today?**

   _____
   _____

Prayers

Today is _____ S M T W TH F S

1. **What can I do to grow my relationship with God today?**
   - ☐ Read the Bible
   - ☐ Pray alone
   - ☐ Pray with a friend, family member, or spouse
   - ☐ Share my faith
   - ☐ Listen to and/or sing to Christian music
   - ☐ Write in my prayer journal
   - ☐ Serve others

2. **What can I praise and thank God for today?**

   _____
   _____
   _____
   _____
   _____

3. **What sins did I commit?**

   _____
   _____

4. **Who needs my prayers?**

   _____
   _____
   _____
   _____

5. **What did I learn today?**

   _____
   _____

6. **What adjustments can I make in my life because of what I learned today?**

   _____
   _____

Prayers

Today is _____ S M T W TH F S

1. **What can I do to grow my relationship with God today?**
   - ☐ Read the Bible
   - ☐ Pray alone
   - ☐ Pray with a friend, family member, or spouse
   - ☐ Share my faith
   - ☐ Listen to and/or sing to Christian music
   - ☐ Write in my prayer journal
   - ☐ Serve others

2. **What can I praise and thank God for today?**

   _____
   _____
   _____
   _____
   _____

3. **What sins did I commit?**

   _____
   _____

4. **Who needs my prayers?**

   _____
   _____
   _____
   _____
   _____

5. **What did I learn today?**

   _____
   _____

6. **What adjustments can I make in my life because of what I learned today?**

   _____
   _____

Prayers

Today is _____ S M T W TH F S

1. **What can I do to grow my relationship with God today?**
   - ☐ Read the Bible
   - ☐ Pray alone
   - ☐ Pray with a friend, family member, or spouse
   - ☐ Share my faith
   - ☐ Listen to and/or sing to Christian music
   - ☐ Write in my prayer journal
   - ☐ Serve others

2. **What can I praise and thank God for today?**

   _____
   _____
   _____
   _____
   _____

3. **What sins did I commit?**

   _____
   _____

4. **Who needs my prayers?**

   _____
   _____
   _____
   _____
   _____

5. **What did I learn today?**

   _____
   _____

6. **What adjustments can I make in my life because of what I learned today?**

   _____
   _____

Prayers

Today is _____ S M T W TH F S

1. **What can I do to grow my relationship with God today?**
   - ☐ Read the Bible
   - ☐ Pray alone
   - ☐ Pray with a friend, family member, or spouse
   - ☐ Share my faith
   - ☐ Listen to and/or sing to Christian music
   - ☐ Write in my prayer journal
   - ☐ Serve others

2. **What can I praise and thank God for today?**

   _____
   _____
   _____
   _____
   _____

3. **What sins did I commit?**

   _____
   _____

4. **Who needs my prayers?**

   _____
   _____
   _____
   _____
   _____

5. **What did I learn today?**

   _____
   _____

6. **What adjustments can I make in my life because of what I learned today?**

   _____
   _____

Prayers

Today is _____ S M T W TH F S

1. **What can I do to grow my relationship with God today?**
   ☐ Read the Bible
   ☐ Pray alone
   ☐ Pray with a friend, family member, or spouse
   ☐ Share my faith
   ☐ Listen to and/or sing to Christian music
   ☐ Write in my prayer journal
   ☐ Serve others

2. **What can I praise and thank God for today?**

   _____
   _____
   _____
   _____
   _____

3. **What sins did I commit?**

   _____
   _____

4. **Who needs my prayers?**

   _____
   _____
   _____
   _____

5. **What did I learn today?**

   _____
   _____

6. **What adjustments can I make in my life because of what I learned today?**

   _____
   _____

Prayers

Today is _____ S M T W TH F S

1. **What can I do to grow my relationship with God today?**
   - ☐ Read the Bible
   - ☐ Pray alone
   - ☐ Pray with a friend, family member, or spouse
   - ☐ Share my faith
   - ☐ Listen to and/or sing to Christian music
   - ☐ Write in my prayer journal
   - ☐ Serve others

2. **What can I praise and thank God for today?**

   _____
   _____
   _____
   _____
   _____

3. **What sins did I commit?**

   _____
   _____

4. **Who needs my prayers?**

   _____
   _____
   _____
   _____
   _____

5. **What did I learn today?**

   _____
   _____

6. **What adjustments can I make in my life because of what I learned today?**

   _____
   _____

Prayers

Today is _____ S M T W TH F S

1. **What can I do to grow my relationship with God today?**
   - ☐ Read the Bible
   - ☐ Pray alone
   - ☐ Pray with a friend, family member, or spouse
   - ☐ Share my faith
   - ☐ Listen to and/or sing to Christian music
   - ☐ Write in my prayer journal
   - ☐ Serve others

2. **What can I praise and thank God for today?**

   _____
   _____
   _____
   _____
   _____

3. **What sins did I commit?**

   _____
   _____

4. **Who needs my prayers?**

   _____
   _____
   _____
   _____
   _____

5. **What did I learn today?**

   _____
   _____

6. **What adjustments can I make in my life because of what I learned today?**

   _____
   _____

Prayers

Today is _____ S M T W TH F S

1. **What can I do to grow my relationship with God today?**
   - ☐ Read the Bible
   - ☐ Pray alone
   - ☐ Pray with a friend, family member, or spouse
   - ☐ Share my faith
   - ☐ Listen to and/or sing to Christian music
   - ☐ Write in my prayer journal
   - ☐ Serve others

2. **What can I praise and thank God for today?**

   _____
   _____
   _____
   _____
   _____

3. **What sins did I commit?**

   _____
   _____

4. **Who needs my prayers?**

   _____
   _____
   _____
   _____

5. **What did I learn today?**

   _____
   _____

6. **What adjustments can I make in my life because of what I learned today?**

   _____
   _____

Prayers

Today is _____ S M T W TH F S

1. **What can I do to grow my relationship with God today?**
   - ☐ Read the Bible
   - ☐ Pray alone
   - ☐ Pray with a friend, family member, or spouse
   - ☐ Share my faith
   - ☐ Listen to and/or sing to Christian music
   - ☐ Write in my prayer journal
   - ☐ Serve others

2. **What can I praise and thank God for today?**

   _____
   _____
   _____
   _____
   _____

3. **What sins did I commit?**

   _____
   _____

4. **Who needs my prayers?**

   _____
   _____
   _____
   _____
   _____

5. **What did I learn today?**

   _____
   _____

6. **What adjustments can I make in my life because of what I learned today?**

   _____
   _____

Prayers

Today is _____ S M T W TH F S

1. **What can I do to grow my relationship with God today?**
   - ☐ Read the Bible
   - ☐ Pray alone
   - ☐ Pray with a friend, family member, or spouse
   - ☐ Share my faith
   - ☐ Listen to and/or sing to Christian music
   - ☐ Write in my prayer journal
   - ☐ Serve others

2. **What can I praise and thank God for today?**

   _____
   _____
   _____
   _____
   _____

3. **What sins did I commit?**

   _____
   _____

4. **Who needs my prayers?**

   _____
   _____
   _____
   _____
   _____

5. **What did I learn today?**

   _____
   _____

6. **What adjustments can I make in my life because of what I learned today?**

   _____
   _____

Prayers

Today is _____ S   M   T   W   TH   F   S

1. **What can I do to grow my relationship with God today?**
   - ☐ Read the Bible
   - ☐ Pray alone
   - ☐ Pray with a friend, family member, or spouse
   - ☐ Share my faith
   - ☐ Listen to and/or sing to Christian music
   - ☐ Write in my prayer journal
   - ☐ Serve others

2. **What can I praise and thank God for today?**

   _____
   _____
   _____
   _____
   _____

3. **What sins did I commit?**

   _____
   _____

4. **Who needs my prayers?**

   _____
   _____
   _____
   _____
   _____

5. **What did I learn today?**

   _____
   _____

6. **What adjustments can I make in my life because of what I learned today?**

   _____
   _____

Prayers

Today is _____ S M T W TH F S

1. **What can I do to grow my relationship with God today?**
   - ☐ Read the Bible
   - ☐ Pray alone
   - ☐ Pray with a friend, family member, or spouse
   - ☐ Share my faith
   - ☐ Listen to and/or sing to Christian music
   - ☐ Write in my prayer journal
   - ☐ Serve others

2. **What can I praise and thank God for today?**

   _____

   _____

   _____

   _____

   _____

3. **What sins did I commit?**

   _____

   _____

4. **Who needs my prayers?**

   _____

   _____

   _____

   _____

   _____

5. **What did I learn today?**

   _____

   _____

6. **What adjustments can I make in my life because of what I learned today?**

   _____

   _____

Prayers

Today is _____ S M T W TH F S

1. **What can I do to grow my relationship with God today?**
   - ☐ Read the Bible
   - ☐ Pray alone
   - ☐ Pray with a friend, family member, or spouse
   - ☐ Share my faith
   - ☐ Listen to and/or sing to Christian music
   - ☐ Write in my prayer journal
   - ☐ Serve others

2. **What can I praise and thank God for today?**

   _____
   _____
   _____
   _____
   _____

3. **What sins did I commit?**

   _____
   _____

4. **Who needs my prayers?**

   _____
   _____
   _____
   _____

5. **What did I learn today?**

   _____
   _____

6. **What adjustments can I make in my life because of what I learned today?**

   _____
   _____

Prayers

Today is _____ S M T W TH F S

1. **What can I do to grow my relationship with God today?**
   - ☐ Read the Bible
   - ☐ Pray alone
   - ☐ Pray with a friend, family member, or spouse
   - ☐ Share my faith
   - ☐ Listen to and/or sing to Christian music
   - ☐ Write in my prayer journal
   - ☐ Serve others

2. **What can I praise and thank God for today?**

   _____
   _____
   _____
   _____
   _____

3. **What sins did I commit?**

   _____
   _____

4. **Who needs my prayers?**

   _____
   _____
   _____
   _____
   _____

5. **What did I learn today?**

   _____
   _____

6. **What adjustments can I make in my life because of what I learned today?**

   _____
   _____

Prayers

Today is _____ S M T W TH F S

1. **What can I do to grow my relationship with God today?**
   - ☐ Read the Bible
   - ☐ Pray alone
   - ☐ Pray with a friend, family member, or spouse
   - ☐ Share my faith
   - ☐ Listen to and/or sing to Christian music
   - ☐ Write in my prayer journal
   - ☐ Serve others

2. **What can I praise and thank God for today?**

   _____
   _____
   _____
   _____
   _____

3. **What sins did I commit?**

   _____
   _____

4. **Who needs my prayers?**

   _____
   _____
   _____
   _____
   _____

5. **What did I learn today?**

   _____
   _____

6. **What adjustments can I make in my life because of what I learned today?**

   _____
   _____

Prayers

Today is _____ S M T W TH F S

1. **What can I do to grow my relationship with God today?**
   - ☐ Read the Bible
   - ☐ Pray alone
   - ☐ Pray with a friend, family member, or spouse
   - ☐ Share my faith
   - ☐ Listen to and/or sing to Christian music
   - ☐ Write in my prayer journal
   - ☐ Serve others

2. **What can I praise and thank God for today?**

   _____
   _____
   _____
   _____
   _____

3. **What sins did I commit?**

   _____
   _____

4. **Who needs my prayers?**

   _____
   _____
   _____
   _____
   _____

5. **What did I learn today?**

   _____
   _____

6. **What adjustments can I make in my life because of what I learned today?**

   _____
   _____

Prayers

Today is _____ S M T W TH F S

1. **What can I do to grow my relationship with God today?**
   - ☐ Read the Bible
   - ☐ Pray alone
   - ☐ Pray with a friend, family member, or spouse
   - ☐ Share my faith
   - ☐ Listen to and/or sing to Christian music
   - ☐ Write in my prayer journal
   - ☐ Serve others

2. **What can I praise and thank God for today?**

   _____
   _____
   _____
   _____
   _____

3. **What sins did I commit?**

   _____
   _____

4. **Who needs my prayers?**

   _____
   _____
   _____
   _____
   _____

5. **What did I learn today?**

   _____
   _____

6. **What adjustments can I make in my life because of what I learned today?**

   _____
   _____

Prayers

Today is _____ S M T W TH F S

1. **What can I do to grow my relationship with God today?**
   - ☐ Read the Bible
   - ☐ Pray alone
   - ☐ Pray with a friend, family member, or spouse
   - ☐ Share my faith
   - ☐ Listen to and/or sing to Christian music
   - ☐ Write in my prayer journal
   - ☐ Serve others

2. **What can I praise and thank God for today?**

   _____
   _____
   _____
   _____
   _____

3. **What sins did I commit?**

   _____
   _____

4. **Who needs my prayers?**

   _____
   _____
   _____
   _____

5. **What did I learn today?**

   _____
   _____

6. **What adjustments can I make in my life because of what I learned today?**

   _____
   _____

Prayers

Today is _____ S M T W TH F S

1. **What can I do to grow my relationship with God today?**
   - ☐ Read the Bible
   - ☐ Pray alone
   - ☐ Pray with a friend, family member, or spouse
   - ☐ Share my faith
   - ☐ Listen to and/or sing to Christian music
   - ☐ Write in my prayer journal
   - ☐ Serve others

2. **What can I praise and thank God for today?**

   _____
   _____
   _____
   _____
   _____

3. **What sins did I commit?**

   _____
   _____

4. **Who needs my prayers?**

   _____
   _____
   _____
   _____
   _____

5. **What did I learn today?**

   _____
   _____

6. **What adjustments can I make in my life because of what I learned today?**

   _____
   _____

Prayers

Today is _____ S M T W TH F S

1. **What can I do to grow my relationship with God today?**
   - ☐ Read the Bible
   - ☐ Pray alone
   - ☐ Pray with a friend, family member, or spouse
   - ☐ Share my faith
   - ☐ Listen to and/or sing to Christian music
   - ☐ Write in my prayer journal
   - ☐ Serve others

2. **What can I praise and thank God for today?**

   _____
   _____
   _____
   _____
   _____

3. **What sins did I commit?**

   _____
   _____

4. **Who needs my prayers?**

   _____
   _____
   _____
   _____
   _____

5. **What did I learn today?**

   _____
   _____

6. **What adjustments can I make in my life because of what I learned today?**

   _____
   _____

Prayers

Today is _____ S M T W TH F S

1. **What can I do to grow my relationship with God today?**
   - ☐ Read the Bible
   - ☐ Pray alone
   - ☐ Pray with a friend, family member, or spouse
   - ☐ Share my faith
   - ☐ Listen to and/or sing to Christian music
   - ☐ Write in my prayer journal
   - ☐ Serve others

2. **What can I praise and thank God for today?**

   _____
   _____
   _____
   _____
   _____

3. **What sins did I commit?**

   _____
   _____

4. **Who needs my prayers?**

   _____
   _____
   _____
   _____
   _____

5. **What did I learn today?**

   _____
   _____

6. **What adjustments can I make in my life because of what I learned today?**

   _____
   _____

Prayers

Today is _____ S M T W TH F S

1. **What can I do to grow my relationship with God today?**
   ☐ Read the Bible
   ☐ Pray alone
   ☐ Pray with a friend, family member, or spouse
   ☐ Share my faith
   ☐ Listen to and/or sing to Christian music
   ☐ Write in my prayer journal
   ☐ Serve others

2. **What can I praise and thank God for today?**

   _____
   _____
   _____
   _____
   _____

3. **What sins did I commit?**

   _____
   _____

4. **Who needs my prayers?**

   _____
   _____
   _____
   _____

5. **What did I learn today?**

   _____
   _____

6. **What adjustments can I make in my life because of what I learned today?**

   _____
   _____

Prayers

Today is _____ S M T W TH F S

1. **What can I do to grow my relationship with God today?**
   - ☐ Read the Bible
   - ☐ Pray alone
   - ☐ Pray with a friend, family member, or spouse
   - ☐ Share my faith
   - ☐ Listen to and/or sing to Christian music
   - ☐ Write in my prayer journal
   - ☐ Serve others

2. **What can I praise and thank God for today?**

   _____
   _____
   _____
   _____
   _____

3. **What sins did I commit?**

   _____
   _____

4. **Who needs my prayers?**

   _____
   _____
   _____
   _____
   _____

5. **What did I learn today?**

   _____
   _____

6. **What adjustments can I make in my life because of what I learned today?**

   _____
   _____

Prayers

Today is _____

1. **What can I do to grow my relationship with God today?**
   - ☐ Read the Bible
   - ☐ Pray alone
   - ☐ Pray with a friend, family member, or spouse
   - ☐ Share my faith
   - ☐ Listen to and/or sing to Christian music
   - ☐ Write in my prayer journal
   - ☐ Serve others

2. **What can I praise and thank God for today?**

   _____
   _____
   _____
   _____
   _____

3. **What sins did I commit?**

   _____
   _____

4. **Who needs my prayers?**

   _____
   _____
   _____
   _____

5. **What did I learn today?**

   _____
   _____

6. **What adjustments can I make in my life because of what I learned today?**

   _____
   _____

Prayers

Month in Review

What specific actions did I take toward meeting my goals?

1.
2.
3.

What did I learn this month? How did God guide me? How did God use me to bless others and to glorify Him?

_____

_____

_____

_____

_____

_____

_____

_____

_____

_____

_____

What adjustments can I make in my life because of what I learned this month?

_____

_____

_____

_____

_____

_____

_____

_____

_____

_____

_____

_____

Spiritual Goals for the Month of

_____

What are my three spiritual goals for this month?

1.
2.
3.

Why do I want to achieve these goals?

1. _____
2. _____
3. _____
4. _____
5. _____

What obstacles do I anticipate?

_____
_____

How will I overcome these obstacles? What support do I need (prayer, scripture, Bible study, a spiritual director, a Christian friend, etc.)?

_____
_____
_____
_____
_____

How will achieving these goals help me glorify God?

_____
_____
_____
_____
_____

Today is _____ S M T W TH F S

1. **What can I do to grow my relationship with God today?**
   - ☐ Read the Bible
   - ☐ Pray alone
   - ☐ Pray with a friend, family member, or spouse
   - ☐ Share my faith
   - ☐ Listen to and/or sing to Christian music
   - ☐ Write in my prayer journal
   - ☐ Serve others

2. **What can I praise and thank God for today?**

   _____
   _____
   _____
   _____
   _____

3. **What sins did I commit?**

   _____
   _____

4. **Who needs my prayers?**

   _____
   _____
   _____
   _____
   _____

5. **What did I learn today?**

   _____
   _____

6. **What adjustments can I make in my life because of what I learned today?**

   _____
   _____

Prayers

Today is _____ S M T W TH F S

1. **What can I do to grow my relationship with God today?**
   ☐ Read the Bible
   ☐ Pray alone
   ☐ Pray with a friend, family
   member, or spouse
   ☐ Share my faith
   ☐ Listen to and/or sing
   to Christian music
   ☐ Write in my prayer journal
   ☐ Serve others

2. **What can I praise and thank God for today?**

   _____
   _____
   _____
   _____
   _____

3. **What sins did I commit?**

   _____
   _____

4. **Who needs my prayers?**

   _____
   _____
   _____
   _____

5. **What did I learn today?**

   _____
   _____

6. **What adjustments can I make in my life because of what I learned today?**

   _____
   _____

Prayers

Today is _____ S M T W TH F S

1. **What can I do to grow my relationship with God today?**
   - ☐ Read the Bible
   - ☐ Pray alone
   - ☐ Pray with a friend, family member, or spouse
   - ☐ Share my faith
   - ☐ Listen to and/or sing to Christian music
   - ☐ Write in my prayer journal
   - ☐ Serve others

2. **What can I praise and thank God for today?**

   _____
   _____
   _____
   _____
   _____

3. **What sins did I commit?**

   _____
   _____

4. **Who needs my prayers?**

   _____
   _____
   _____
   _____

5. **What did I learn today?**

   _____
   _____

6. **What adjustments can I make in my life because of what I learned today?**

   _____
   _____

Prayers

Today is _____ S M T W TH F S

1. **What can I do to grow my relationship with God today?**
   - ☐ Read the Bible
   - ☐ Pray alone
   - ☐ Pray with a friend, family member, or spouse
   - ☐ Share my faith
   - ☐ Listen to and/or sing to Christian music
   - ☐ Write in my prayer journal
   - ☐ Serve others

2. **What can I praise and thank God for today?**

   _____
   _____
   _____
   _____
   _____

3. **What sins did I commit?**

   _____
   _____

4. **Who needs my prayers?**

   _____
   _____
   _____
   _____
   _____

5. **What did I learn today?**

   _____
   _____

6. **What adjustments can I make in my life because of what I learned today?**

   _____
   _____

Prayers

Today is _____ S M T W TH F S

1. **What can I do to grow my relationship with God today?**
   - ☐ Read the Bible
   - ☐ Pray alone
   - ☐ Pray with a friend, family member, or spouse
   - ☐ Share my faith
   - ☐ Listen to and/or sing to Christian music
   - ☐ Write in my prayer journal
   - ☐ Serve others

2. **What can I praise and thank God for today?**

   _____
   _____
   _____
   _____
   _____

3. **What sins did I commit?**

   _____
   _____

4. **Who needs my prayers?**

   _____
   _____
   _____
   _____
   _____

5. **What did I learn today?**

   _____
   _____

6. **What adjustments can I make in my life because of what I learned today?**

   _____
   _____

Prayers

Today is _____ S M T W TH F S

1. **What can I do to grow my relationship with God today?**
   - ☐ Read the Bible
   - ☐ Pray alone
   - ☐ Pray with a friend, family member, or spouse
   - ☐ Share my faith
   - ☐ Listen to and/or sing to Christian music
   - ☐ Write in my prayer journal
   - ☐ Serve others

2. **What can I praise and thank God for today?**

   _____
   _____
   _____
   _____
   _____

3. **What sins did I commit?**

   _____
   _____

4. **Who needs my prayers?**

   _____
   _____
   _____
   _____
   _____

5. **What did I learn today?**

   _____
   _____

6. **What adjustments can I make in my life because of what I learned today?**

   _____
   _____

Prayers

Today is _____ S M T W TH F S

1. **What can I do to grow my relationship with God today?**
   - ☐ Read the Bible
   - ☐ Pray alone
   - ☐ Pray with a friend, family member, or spouse
   - ☐ Share my faith
   - ☐ Listen to and/or sing to Christian music
   - ☐ Write in my prayer journal
   - ☐ Serve others

2. **What can I praise and thank God for today?**

   _____
   _____
   _____
   _____
   _____

3. **What sins did I commit?**

   _____
   _____

4. **Who needs my prayers?**

   _____
   _____
   _____
   _____
   _____

5. **What did I learn today?**

   _____
   _____

6. **What adjustments can I make in my life because of what I learned today?**

   _____
   _____

Prayers

Today is _____ S M T W TH F S

1. **What can I do to grow my relationship with God today?**
   ☐ Read the Bible
   ☐ Pray alone
   ☐ Pray with a friend, family member, or spouse
   ☐ Share my faith
   ☐ Listen to and/or sing to Christian music
   ☐ Write in my prayer journal
   ☐ Serve others

2. **What can I praise and thank God for today?**

   _____
   _____
   _____
   _____
   _____

3. **What sins did I commit?**

   _____
   _____

4. **Who needs my prayers?**

   _____
   _____
   _____
   _____
   _____

5. **What did I learn today?**

   _____
   _____

6. **What adjustments can I make in my life because of what I learned today?**

   _____
   _____

Prayers

Today is _____ S M T W TH F S

1. **What can I do to grow my relationship with God today?**
   - ☐ Read the Bible
   - ☐ Pray alone
   - ☐ Pray with a friend, family member, or spouse
   - ☐ Share my faith
   - ☐ Listen to and/or sing to Christian music
   - ☐ Write in my prayer journal
   - ☐ Serve others

2. **What can I praise and thank God for today?**

   _____
   _____
   _____
   _____
   _____

3. **What sins did I commit?**

   _____
   _____

4. **Who needs my prayers?**

   _____
   _____
   _____
   _____
   _____

5. **What did I learn today?**

   _____
   _____

6. **What adjustments can I make in my life because of what I learned today?**

   _____
   _____

Prayers

Today is _____ S M T W TH F S

1. **What can I do to grow my relationship with God today?**
   - ☐ Read the Bible
   - ☐ Pray alone
   - ☐ Pray with a friend, family member, or spouse
   - ☐ Share my faith
   - ☐ Listen to and/or sing to Christian music
   - ☐ Write in my prayer journal
   - ☐ Serve others

2. **What can I praise and thank God for today?**

   _____

   _____

   _____

   _____

   _____

3. **What sins did I commit?**

   _____

   _____

4. **Who needs my prayers?**

   _____

   _____

   _____

   _____

5. **What did I learn today?**

   _____

   _____

6. **What adjustments can I make in my life because of what I learned today?**

   _____

   _____

Prayers

Today is _____ S M T W TH F S

1. **What can I do to grow my relationship with God today?**
   - ☐ Read the Bible
   - ☐ Pray alone
   - ☐ Pray with a friend, family member, or spouse
   - ☐ Share my faith
   - ☐ Listen to and/or sing to Christian music
   - ☐ Write in my prayer journal
   - ☐ Serve others

2. **What can I praise and thank God for today?**

   _____

   _____

   _____

   _____

   _____

3. **What sins did I commit?**

   _____

   _____

4. **Who needs my prayers?**

   _____

   _____

   _____

   _____

   _____

5. **What did I learn today?**

   _____

   _____

6. **What adjustments can I make in my life because of what I learned today?**

   _____

   _____

Prayers

Today is _____ S M T W TH F S

1. **What can I do to grow my relationship with God today?**
   - ☐ Read the Bible
   - ☐ Pray alone
   - ☐ Pray with a friend, family member, or spouse
   - ☐ Share my faith
   - ☐ Listen to and/or sing to Christian music
   - ☐ Write in my prayer journal
   - ☐ Serve others

2. **What can I praise and thank God for today?**

   _____

   _____

   _____

   _____

   _____

3. **What sins did I commit?**

   _____

   _____

4. **Who needs my prayers?**

   _____

   _____

   _____

   _____

   _____

5. **What did I learn today?**

   _____

   _____

6. **What adjustments can I make in my life because of what I learned today?**

   _____

   _____

Prayers

Today is _____ S M T W TH F S

1. **What can I do to grow my relationship with God today?**
   - ☐ Read the Bible
   - ☐ Pray alone
   - ☐ Pray with a friend, family member, or spouse
   - ☐ Share my faith
   - ☐ Listen to and/or sing to Christian music
   - ☐ Write in my prayer journal
   - ☐ Serve others

2. **What can I praise and thank God for today?**

   _____
   _____
   _____
   _____
   _____

3. **What sins did I commit?**

   _____
   _____

4. **Who needs my prayers?**

   _____
   _____
   _____
   _____

5. **What did I learn today?**

   _____
   _____

6. **What adjustments can I make in my life because of what I learned today?**

   _____
   _____

Prayers

Today is _____ S M T W TH F S

1. **What can I do to grow my relationship with God today?**
   ☐ Read the Bible
   ☐ Pray alone
   ☐ Pray with a friend, family member, or spouse
   ☐ Share my faith
   ☐ Listen to and/or sing to Christian music
   ☐ Write in my prayer journal
   ☐ Serve others

2. **What can I praise and thank God for today?**

   _____
   _____
   _____
   _____
   _____

3. **What sins did I commit?**

   _____
   _____

4. **Who needs my prayers?**

   _____
   _____
   _____
   _____

5. **What did I learn today?**

   _____
   _____

6. **What adjustments can I make in my life because of what I learned today?**

   _____
   _____

Prayers

Today is _____

1. **What can I do to grow my relationship with God today?**
   ☐ Read the Bible
   ☐ Pray alone
   ☐ Pray with a friend, family
      member, or spouse
   ☐ Share my faith

   ☐ Listen to and/or sing
      to Christian music
   ☐ Write in my prayer journal
   ☐ Serve others

2. **What can I praise and thank God for today?**

   _____
   _____
   _____
   _____
   _____

3. **What sins did I commit?**

   _____
   _____

4. **Who needs my prayers?**

   _____
   _____
   _____
   _____
   _____

5. **What did I learn today?**

   _____
   _____

6. **What adjustments can I make in my life because of what I learned today?**

   _____
   _____

Prayers

Today is _____ S M T W TH F S

1. **What can I do to grow my relationship with God today?**
   - ☐ Read the Bible
   - ☐ Pray alone
   - ☐ Pray with a friend, family member, or spouse
   - ☐ Share my faith
   - ☐ Listen to and/or sing to Christian music
   - ☐ Write in my prayer journal
   - ☐ Serve others

2. **What can I praise and thank God for today?**

   _____
   _____
   _____
   _____
   _____

3. **What sins did I commit?**

   _____
   _____

4. **Who needs my prayers?**

   _____
   _____
   _____
   _____
   _____

5. **What did I learn today?**

   _____
   _____

6. **What adjustments can I make in my life because of what I learned today?**

   _____
   _____

Prayers

Today is _____ S M T W TH F S

1. **What can I do to grow my relationship with God today?**
   - ☐ Read the Bible
   - ☐ Pray alone
   - ☐ Pray with a friend, family member, or spouse
   - ☐ Share my faith
   - ☐ Listen to and/or sing to Christian music
   - ☐ Write in my prayer journal
   - ☐ Serve others

2. **What can I praise and thank God for today?**

   _____
   _____
   _____
   _____
   _____

3. **What sins did I commit?**

   _____
   _____

4. **Who needs my prayers?**

   _____
   _____
   _____
   _____

5. **What did I learn today?**

   _____
   _____

6. **What adjustments can I make in my life because of what I learned today?**

   _____
   _____

Prayers

Today is _____ S M T W TH F S

1. **What can I do to grow my relationship with God today?**
   - ☐ Read the Bible
   - ☐ Pray alone
   - ☐ Pray with a friend, family member, or spouse
   - ☐ Share my faith
   - ☐ Listen to and/or sing to Christian music
   - ☐ Write in my prayer journal
   - ☐ Serve others

2. **What can I praise and thank God for today?**

   _____
   _____
   _____
   _____
   _____

3. **What sins did I commit?**

   _____
   _____

4. **Who needs my prayers?**

   _____
   _____
   _____
   _____
   _____

5. **What did I learn today?**

   _____
   _____

6. **What adjustments can I make in my life because of what I learned today?**

   _____
   _____

Prayers

Today is _____ S M T W TH F S

1. **What can I do to grow my relationship with God today?**
   - ☐ Read the Bible
   - ☐ Pray alone
   - ☐ Pray with a friend, family member, or spouse
   - ☐ Share my faith
   - ☐ Listen to and/or sing to Christian music
   - ☐ Write in my prayer journal
   - ☐ Serve others

2. **What can I praise and thank God for today?**

   _____
   _____
   _____
   _____
   _____

3. **What sins did I commit?**

   _____
   _____

4. **Who needs my prayers?**

   _____
   _____
   _____
   _____
   _____

5. **What did I learn today?**

   _____
   _____

6. **What adjustments can I make in my life because of what I learned today?**

   _____
   _____

Prayers

Today is _____ S M T W TH F S

1. **What can I do to grow my relationship with God today?**
   - ☐ Read the Bible
   - ☐ Pray alone
   - ☐ Pray with a friend, family member, or spouse
   - ☐ Share my faith
   - ☐ Listen to and/or sing to Christian music
   - ☐ Write in my prayer journal
   - ☐ Serve others

2. **What can I praise and thank God for today?**

   _____
   _____
   _____
   _____
   _____

3. **What sins did I commit?**

   _____
   _____

4. **Who needs my prayers?**

   _____
   _____
   _____
   _____

5. **What did I learn today?**

   _____
   _____

6. **What adjustments can I make in my life because of what I learned today?**

   _____
   _____

Prayers

Today is _____ S M T W TH F S

1. **What can I do to grow my relationship with God today?**
   - ☐ Read the Bible
   - ☐ Pray alone
   - ☐ Pray with a friend, family member, or spouse
   - ☐ Share my faith
   - ☐ Listen to and/or sing to Christian music
   - ☐ Write in my prayer journal
   - ☐ Serve others

2. **What can I praise and thank God for today?**

   _____
   _____
   _____
   _____
   _____

3. **What sins did I commit?**

   _____
   _____

4. **Who needs my prayers?**

   _____
   _____
   _____
   _____

5. **What did I learn today?**

   _____
   _____

6. **What adjustments can I make in my life because of what I learned today?**

   _____
   _____

Prayers

Today is _____ S M T W TH F S

1. **What can I do to grow my relationship with God today?**
   ☐ Read the Bible
   ☐ Pray alone
   ☐ Pray with a friend, family member, or spouse
   ☐ Share my faith
   ☐ Listen to and/or sing to Christian music
   ☐ Write in my prayer journal
   ☐ Serve others

2. **What can I praise and thank God for today?**

   _____
   _____
   _____
   _____
   _____

3. **What sins did I commit?**

   _____
   _____

4. **Who needs my prayers?**

   _____
   _____
   _____
   _____

5. **What did I learn today?**

   _____
   _____

6. **What adjustments can I make in my life because of what I learned today?**

   _____
   _____

Prayers

Today is _____ S M T W TH F S

1. **What can I do to grow my relationship with God today?**
   - ☐ Read the Bible
   - ☐ Pray alone
   - ☐ Pray with a friend, family member, or spouse
   - ☐ Share my faith
   - ☐ Listen to and/or sing to Christian music
   - ☐ Write in my prayer journal
   - ☐ Serve others

2. **What can I praise and thank God for today?**

   _____
   _____
   _____
   _____
   _____

3. **What sins did I commit?**

   _____
   _____

4. **Who needs my prayers?**

   _____
   _____
   _____
   _____

5. **What did I learn today?**

   _____
   _____

6. **What adjustments can I make in my life because of what I learned today?**

   _____
   _____

Prayers

Today is _____ S   M   T   W   TH   F   S

1. **What can I do to grow my relationship with God today?**
   - ☐ Read the Bible
   - ☐ Pray alone
   - ☐ Pray with a friend, family member, or spouse
   - ☐ Share my faith
   - ☐ Listen to and/or sing to Christian music
   - ☐ Write in my prayer journal
   - ☐ Serve others

2. **What can I praise and thank God for today?**

   _____
   _____
   _____
   _____
   _____

3. **What sins did I commit?**

   _____
   _____

4. **Who needs my prayers?**

   _____
   _____
   _____
   _____
   _____

5. **What did I learn today?**

   _____
   _____

6. **What adjustments can I make in my life because of what I learned today?**

   _____
   _____

Prayers

Today is _____ S   M   T   W   TH   F   S

1. **What can I do to grow my relationship with God today?**
    - ☐ Read the Bible
    - ☐ Pray alone
    - ☐ Pray with a friend, family member, or spouse
    - ☐ Share my faith
    - ☐ Listen to and/or sing to Christian music
    - ☐ Write in my prayer journal
    - ☐ Serve others

2. **What can I praise and thank God for today?**

    _____
    _____
    _____
    _____
    _____

3. **What sins did I commit?**

    _____
    _____

4. **Who needs my prayers?**

    _____
    _____
    _____
    _____
    _____

5. **What did I learn today?**

    _____
    _____

6. **What adjustments can I make in my life because of what I learned today?**

    _____
    _____

Prayers

Today is _____ S M T W TH F S

1. **What can I do to grow my relationship with God today?**
   - ☐ Read the Bible
   - ☐ Pray alone
   - ☐ Pray with a friend, family member, or spouse
   - ☐ Share my faith
   - ☐ Listen to and/or sing to Christian music
   - ☐ Write in my prayer journal
   - ☐ Serve others

2. **What can I praise and thank God for today?**

   _____
   _____
   _____
   _____
   _____

3. **What sins did I commit?**

   _____
   _____

4. **Who needs my prayers?**

   _____
   _____
   _____
   _____
   _____

5. **What did I learn today?**

   _____
   _____

6. **What adjustments can I make in my life because of what I learned today?**

   _____
   _____

Prayers

Today is _____ S M T W TH F S

1. **What can I do to grow my relationship with God today?**
   - ☐ Read the Bible
   - ☐ Pray alone
   - ☐ Pray with a friend, family member, or spouse
   - ☐ Share my faith
   - ☐ Listen to and/or sing to Christian music
   - ☐ Write in my prayer journal
   - ☐ Serve others

2. **What can I praise and thank God for today?**

   _____
   _____
   _____
   _____
   _____

3. **What sins did I commit?**

   _____
   _____

4. **Who needs my prayers?**

   _____
   _____
   _____
   _____

5. **What did I learn today?**

   _____
   _____

6. **What adjustments can I make in my life because of what I learned today?**

   _____
   _____

Prayers

Today is _____ S M T W TH F S

1. **What can I do to grow my relationship with God today?**
   - ☐ Read the Bible
   - ☐ Pray alone
   - ☐ Pray with a friend, family member, or spouse
   - ☐ Share my faith
   - ☐ Listen to and/or sing to Christian music
   - ☐ Write in my prayer journal
   - ☐ Serve others

2. **What can I praise and thank God for today?**

   _____
   _____
   _____
   _____
   _____

3. **What sins did I commit?**

   _____
   _____

4. **Who needs my prayers?**

   _____
   _____
   _____
   _____
   _____

5. **What did I learn today?**

   _____
   _____

6. **What adjustments can I make in my life because of what I learned today?**

   _____
   _____

Prayers

Today is _____ S M T W TH F S

1. **What can I do to grow my relationship with God today?**
   - ☐ Read the Bible
   - ☐ Pray alone
   - ☐ Pray with a friend, family member, or spouse
   - ☐ Share my faith
   - ☐ Listen to and/or sing to Christian music
   - ☐ Write in my prayer journal
   - ☐ Serve others

2. **What can I praise and thank God for today?**

   _____
   _____
   _____
   _____
   _____

3. **What sins did I commit?**

   _____
   _____

4. **Who needs my prayers?**

   _____
   _____
   _____
   _____

5. **What did I learn today?**

   _____
   _____

6. **What adjustments can I make in my life because of what I learned today?**

   _____
   _____

Prayers

Today is _____ S M T W TH F S

1. **What can I do to grow my relationship with God today?**
   - ☐ Read the Bible
   - ☐ Pray alone
   - ☐ Pray with a friend, family member, or spouse
   - ☐ Share my faith
   - ☐ Listen to and/or sing to Christian music
   - ☐ Write in my prayer journal
   - ☐ Serve others

2. **What can I praise and thank God for today?**

   _____
   _____
   _____
   _____
   _____

3. **What sins did I commit?**

   _____
   _____

4. **Who needs my prayers?**

   _____
   _____
   _____
   _____

5. **What did I learn today?**

   _____
   _____

6. **What adjustments can I make in my life because of what I learned today?**

   _____
   _____

Prayers

Today is _____ S M T W TH F S

1. **What can I do to grow my relationship with God today?**
   - ☐ Read the Bible
   - ☐ Pray alone
   - ☐ Pray with a friend, family member, or spouse
   - ☐ Share my faith
   - ☐ Listen to and/or sing to Christian music
   - ☐ Write in my prayer journal
   - ☐ Serve others

2. **What can I praise and thank God for today?**

   _____
   _____
   _____
   _____
   _____

3. **What sins did I commit?**

   _____
   _____

4. **Who needs my prayers?**

   _____
   _____
   _____
   _____
   _____

5. **What did I learn today?**

   _____
   _____

6. **What adjustments can I make in my life because of what I learned today?**

   _____
   _____

Prayers

Month in Review

What specific actions did I take toward meeting my goals?

1.
2.
3.

What did I learn this month? How did God guide me? How did God use me to bless others and to glorify Him?

_____
_____
_____
_____
_____
_____
_____
_____
_____
_____
_____

What adjustments can I make in my life because of what I learned this month?

_____
_____
_____
_____
_____
_____
_____
_____
_____
_____
_____
_____

Spiritual Goals for the Month of

_____

What are my three spiritual goals for this month?

1.
2.
3.

Why do I want to achieve these goals?

1. _____
2. _____
3. _____
4. _____
5. _____

What obstacles do I anticipate?

_____
_____

How will I overcome these obstacles? What support do I need (prayer, scripture, Bible study, a spiritual director, a Christian friend, etc.)?

_____
_____
_____
_____
_____

How will achieving these goals help me glorify God?

_____
_____
_____
_____
_____

Today is _____ S M T W TH F S

1. **What can I do to grow my relationship with God today?**
   - ☐ Read the Bible
   - ☐ Pray alone
   - ☐ Pray with a friend, family member, or spouse
   - ☐ Share my faith
   - ☐ Listen to and/or sing to Christian music
   - ☐ Write in my prayer journal
   - ☐ Serve others

2. **What can I praise and thank God for today?**

   _____
   _____
   _____
   _____
   _____

3. **What sins did I commit?**

   _____
   _____

4. **Who needs my prayers?**

   _____
   _____
   _____
   _____

5. **What did I learn today?**

   _____
   _____

6. **What adjustments can I make in my life because of what I learned today?**

   _____
   _____

Prayers

Today is _____ S M T W TH F S

1. **What can I do to grow my relationship with God today?**
   - ☐ Read the Bible
   - ☐ Pray alone
   - ☐ Pray with a friend, family member, or spouse
   - ☐ Share my faith
   - ☐ Listen to and/or sing to Christian music
   - ☐ Write in my prayer journal
   - ☐ Serve others

2. **What can I praise and thank God for today?**

   _____
   _____
   _____
   _____
   _____

3. **What sins did I commit?**

   _____
   _____

4. **Who needs my prayers?**

   _____
   _____
   _____
   _____

5. **What did I learn today?**

   _____
   _____

6. **What adjustments can I make in my life because of what I learned today?**

   _____
   _____

Prayers

Today is _____ S M T W TH F S

1. **What can I do to grow my relationship with God today?**
    - ☐ Read the Bible
    - ☐ Pray alone
    - ☐ Pray with a friend, family member, or spouse
    - ☐ Share my faith
    - ☐ Listen to and/or sing to Christian music
    - ☐ Write in my prayer journal
    - ☐ Serve others

2. **What can I praise and thank God for today?**

    _____
    _____
    _____
    _____
    _____

3. **What sins did I commit?**

    _____
    _____

4. **Who needs my prayers?**

    _____
    _____
    _____
    _____

5. **What did I learn today?**

    _____
    _____

6. **What adjustments can I make in my life because of what I learned today?**

    _____
    _____

Prayers

Today is _____ S M T W TH F S

1. **What can I do to grow my relationship with God today?**
   - ☐ Read the Bible
   - ☐ Pray alone
   - ☐ Pray with a friend, family member, or spouse
   - ☐ Share my faith
   - ☐ Listen to and/or sing to Christian music
   - ☐ Write in my prayer journal
   - ☐ Serve others

2. **What can I praise and thank God for today?**

   _____
   _____
   _____
   _____
   _____

3. **What sins did I commit?**

   _____
   _____

4. **Who needs my prayers?**

   _____
   _____
   _____
   _____
   _____

5. **What did I learn today?**

   _____
   _____

6. **What adjustments can I make in my life because of what I learned today?**

   _____
   _____

Prayers

Today is _____ S M T W TH F S

1. **What can I do to grow my relationship with God today?**
   - ☐ Read the Bible
   - ☐ Pray alone
   - ☐ Pray with a friend, family member, or spouse
   - ☐ Share my faith
   - ☐ Listen to and/or sing to Christian music
   - ☐ Write in my prayer journal
   - ☐ Serve others

2. **What can I praise and thank God for today?**

   _____
   _____
   _____
   _____
   _____

3. **What sins did I commit?**

   _____
   _____

4. **Who needs my prayers?**

   _____
   _____
   _____
   _____

5. **What did I learn today?**

   _____
   _____

6. **What adjustments can I make in my life because of what I learned today?**

   _____
   _____

Prayers

Today is _____ S M T W TH F S

1. **What can I do to grow my relationship with God today?**
    ☐ Read the Bible
    ☐ Pray alone
    ☐ Pray with a friend, family member, or spouse
    ☐ Share my faith
    ☐ Listen to and/or sing to Christian music
    ☐ Write in my prayer journal
    ☐ Serve others

2. **What can I praise and thank God for today?**

    _____
    _____
    _____
    _____
    _____

3. **What sins did I commit?**

    _____
    _____

4. **Who needs my prayers?**

    _____
    _____
    _____
    _____
    _____

5. **What did I learn today?**

    _____
    _____

6. **What adjustments can I make in my life because of what I learned today?**

    _____
    _____

Prayers

Today is _____ S M T W TH F S

1. **What can I do to grow my relationship with God today?**
   - ☐ Read the Bible
   - ☐ Pray alone
   - ☐ Pray with a friend, family member, or spouse
   - ☐ Share my faith
   - ☐ Listen to and/or sing to Christian music
   - ☐ Write in my prayer journal
   - ☐ Serve others

2. **What can I praise and thank God for today?**

   _____
   _____
   _____
   _____
   _____

3. **What sins did I commit?**

   _____
   _____

4. **Who needs my prayers?**

   _____
   _____
   _____
   _____

5. **What did I learn today?**

   _____
   _____

6. **What adjustments can I make in my life because of what I learned today?**

   _____
   _____

Prayers

Today is _____ S M T W TH F S

1. **What can I do to grow my relationship with God today?**
   - ☐ Read the Bible
   - ☐ Pray alone
   - ☐ Pray with a friend, family member, or spouse
   - ☐ Share my faith
   - ☐ Listen to and/or sing to Christian music
   - ☐ Write in my prayer journal
   - ☐ Serve others

2. **What can I praise and thank God for today?**

   _____
   _____
   _____
   _____
   _____

3. **What sins did I commit?**

   _____
   _____

4. **Who needs my prayers?**

   _____
   _____
   _____
   _____
   _____

5. **What did I learn today?**

   _____
   _____

6. **What adjustments can I make in my life because of what I learned today?**

   _____
   _____

Prayers

Today is _____ S M T W TH F S

1. **What can I do to grow my relationship with God today?**
   - ☐ Read the Bible
   - ☐ Pray alone
   - ☐ Pray with a friend, family member, or spouse
   - ☐ Share my faith
   - ☐ Listen to and/or sing to Christian music
   - ☐ Write in my prayer journal
   - ☐ Serve others

2. **What can I praise and thank God for today?**

   _____
   _____
   _____
   _____
   _____

3. **What sins did I commit?**

   _____
   _____

4. **Who needs my prayers?**

   _____
   _____
   _____
   _____
   _____

5. **What did I learn today?**

   _____
   _____

6. **What adjustments can I make in my life because of what I learned today?**

   _____
   _____

Prayers

Today is _____ S   M   T   W   TH   F   S

1. **What can I do to grow my relationship with God today?**
   - ☐ Read the Bible
   - ☐ Pray alone
   - ☐ Pray with a friend, family member, or spouse
   - ☐ Share my faith
   - ☐ Listen to and/or sing to Christian music
   - ☐ Write in my prayer journal
   - ☐ Serve others

2. **What can I praise and thank God for today?**

   _____
   _____
   _____
   _____
   _____

3. **What sins did I commit?**

   _____
   _____

4. **Who needs my prayers?**

   _____
   _____
   _____
   _____
   _____

5. **What did I learn today?**

   _____
   _____

6. **What adjustments can I make in my life because of what I learned today?**

   _____
   _____

Prayers

Today is _____ S M T W TH F S

1. **What can I do to grow my relationship with God today?**
   - ☐ Read the Bible
   - ☐ Pray alone
   - ☐ Pray with a friend, family member, or spouse
   - ☐ Share my faith
   - ☐ Listen to and/or sing to Christian music
   - ☐ Write in my prayer journal
   - ☐ Serve others

2. **What can I praise and thank God for today?**

   _____
   _____
   _____
   _____
   _____

3. **What sins did I commit?**

   _____
   _____

4. **Who needs my prayers?**

   _____
   _____
   _____
   _____
   _____

5. **What did I learn today?**

   _____
   _____

6. **What adjustments can I make in my life because of what I learned today?**

   _____
   _____

Prayers

Today is _____ S M T W TH F S

1. **What can I do to grow my relationship with God today?**
   - ☐ Read the Bible
   - ☐ Pray alone
   - ☐ Pray with a friend, family member, or spouse
   - ☐ Share my faith
   - ☐ Listen to and/or sing to Christian music
   - ☐ Write in my prayer journal
   - ☐ Serve others

2. **What can I praise and thank God for today?**

   _____
   _____
   _____
   _____
   _____

3. **What sins did I commit?**

   _____
   _____

4. **Who needs my prayers?**

   _____
   _____
   _____
   _____
   _____

5. **What did I learn today?**

   _____
   _____

6. **What adjustments can I make in my life because of what I learned today?**

   _____
   _____

Prayers

Today is _____ S M T W TH F S

1. **What can I do to grow my relationship with God today?**
   ☐ Read the Bible
   ☐ Pray alone
   ☐ Pray with a friend, family
      member, or spouse
   ☐ Share my faith
   ☐ Listen to and/or sing
      to Christian music
   ☐ Write in my prayer journal
   ☐ Serve others

2. **What can I praise and thank God for today?**

   _____
   _____
   _____
   _____
   _____

3. **What sins did I commit?**

   _____
   _____

4. **Who needs my prayers?**

   _____
   _____
   _____
   _____
   _____

5. **What did I learn today?**

   _____
   _____

6. **What adjustments can I make in my life because of what I learned today?**

   _____
   _____

Prayers

Today is _____ S M T W TH F S

1. **What can I do to grow my relationship with God today?**
   ☐ Read the Bible
   ☐ Pray alone
   ☐ Pray with a friend, family member, or spouse
   ☐ Share my faith
   ☐ Listen to and/or sing to Christian music
   ☐ Write in my prayer journal
   ☐ Serve others

2. **What can I praise and thank God for today?**

   _____
   _____
   _____
   _____
   _____

3. **What sins did I commit?**

   _____
   _____

4. **Who needs my prayers?**

   _____
   _____
   _____
   _____
   _____

5. **What did I learn today?**

   _____
   _____

6. **What adjustments can I make in my life because of what I learned today?**

   _____
   _____

Prayers

Today is _____ S M T W TH F S

1. **What can I do to grow my relationship with God today?**
   - ☐ Read the Bible
   - ☐ Pray alone
   - ☐ Pray with a friend, family member, or spouse
   - ☐ Share my faith
   - ☐ Listen to and/or sing to Christian music
   - ☐ Write in my prayer journal
   - ☐ Serve others

2. **What can I praise and thank God for today?**

   _____
   _____
   _____
   _____
   _____

3. **What sins did I commit?**

   _____
   _____

4. **Who needs my prayers?**

   _____
   _____
   _____
   _____
   _____

5. **What did I learn today?**

   _____
   _____

6. **What adjustments can I make in my life because of what I learned today?**

   _____
   _____

Prayers

Today is _____ S M T W TH F S

1. **What can I do to grow my relationship with God today?**
   - ☐ Read the Bible
   - ☐ Pray alone
   - ☐ Pray with a friend, family member, or spouse
   - ☐ Share my faith
   - ☐ Listen to and/or sing to Christian music
   - ☐ Write in my prayer journal
   - ☐ Serve others

2. **What can I praise and thank God for today?**

   _____
   _____
   _____
   _____
   _____

3. **What sins did I commit?**

   _____
   _____

4. **Who needs my prayers?**

   _____
   _____
   _____
   _____
   _____

5. **What did I learn today?**

   _____
   _____

6. **What adjustments can I make in my life because of what I learned today?**

   _____
   _____

Prayers

Today is _____ S M T W TH F S

1. **What can I do to grow my relationship with God today?**
   ☐ Read the Bible
   ☐ Pray alone
   ☐ Pray with a friend, family member, or spouse
   ☐ Share my faith
   ☐ Listen to and/or sing to Christian music
   ☐ Write in my prayer journal
   ☐ Serve others

2. **What can I praise and thank God for today?**

   _____
   _____
   _____
   _____
   _____

3. **What sins did I commit?**

   _____
   _____

4. **Who needs my prayers?**

   _____
   _____
   _____
   _____

5. **What did I learn today?**

   _____
   _____

6. **What adjustments can I make in my life because of what I learned today?**

   _____
   _____

Prayers

Today is _____ S M T W TH F S

1. **What can I do to grow my relationship with God today?**
   - ☐ Read the Bible
   - ☐ Pray alone
   - ☐ Pray with a friend, family member, or spouse
   - ☐ Share my faith
   - ☐ Listen to and/or sing to Christian music
   - ☐ Write in my prayer journal
   - ☐ Serve others

2. **What can I praise and thank God for today?**

   _____

   _____

   _____

   _____

   _____

3. **What sins did I commit?**

   _____

   _____

4. **Who needs my prayers?**

   _____

   _____

   _____

   _____

   _____

5. **What did I learn today?**

   _____

   _____

6. **What adjustments can I make in my life because of what I learned today?**

   _____

   _____

Prayers

Today is _____ S M T W TH F S

1. **What can I do to grow my relationship with God today?**
   - ☐ Read the Bible
   - ☐ Pray alone
   - ☐ Pray with a friend, family member, or spouse
   - ☐ Share my faith
   - ☐ Listen to and/or sing to Christian music
   - ☐ Write in my prayer journal
   - ☐ Serve others

2. **What can I praise and thank God for today?**

   _____
   _____
   _____
   _____
   _____

3. **What sins did I commit?**

   _____
   _____

4. **Who needs my prayers?**

   _____
   _____
   _____
   _____

5. **What did I learn today?**

   _____
   _____

6. **What adjustments can I make in my life because of what I learned today?**

   _____
   _____

Prayers

Today is _____ S   M   T   W   TH   F   S

1. **What can I do to grow my relationship with God today?**
   - ☐ Read the Bible
   - ☐ Pray alone
   - ☐ Pray with a friend, family member, or spouse
   - ☐ Share my faith
   - ☐ Listen to and/or sing to Christian music
   - ☐ Write in my prayer journal
   - ☐ Serve others

2. **What can I praise and thank God for today?**

   _____

   _____

   _____

   _____

   _____

3. **What sins did I commit?**

   _____

   _____

4. **Who needs my prayers?**

   _____

   _____

   _____

   _____

5. **What did I learn today?**

   _____

   _____

6. **What adjustments can I make in my life because of what I learned today?**

   _____

   _____

Prayers

Today is _____ S M T W TH F S

1. **What can I do to grow my relationship with God today?**
   - ☐ Read the Bible
   - ☐ Pray alone
   - ☐ Pray with a friend, family member, or spouse
   - ☐ Share my faith
   - ☐ Listen to and/or sing to Christian music
   - ☐ Write in my prayer journal
   - ☐ Serve others

2. **What can I praise and thank God for today?**

   _____
   _____
   _____
   _____
   _____

3. **What sins did I commit?**

   _____
   _____

4. **Who needs my prayers?**

   _____
   _____
   _____
   _____
   _____

5. **What did I learn today?**

   _____
   _____

6. **What adjustments can I make in my life because of what I learned today?**

   _____
   _____

Prayers

Today is _____ S M T W TH F S

1. **What can I do to grow my relationship with God today?**
   - ☐ Read the Bible
   - ☐ Pray alone
   - ☐ Pray with a friend, family member, or spouse
   - ☐ Share my faith
   - ☐ Listen to and/or sing to Christian music
   - ☐ Write in my prayer journal
   - ☐ Serve others

2. **What can I praise and thank God for today?**

   _____
   _____
   _____
   _____
   _____

3. **What sins did I commit?**

   _____
   _____

4. **Who needs my prayers?**

   _____
   _____
   _____
   _____

5. **What did I learn today?**

   _____
   _____

6. **What adjustments can I make in my life because of what I learned today?**

   _____
   _____

Prayers

Today is _____ S M T W TH F S

1. **What can I do to grow my relationship with God today?**
   - ☐ Read the Bible
   - ☐ Pray alone
   - ☐ Pray with a friend, family member, or spouse
   - ☐ Share my faith
   - ☐ Listen to and/or sing to Christian music
   - ☐ Write in my prayer journal
   - ☐ Serve others

2. **What can I praise and thank God for today?**

   _____

   _____

   _____

   _____

   _____

3. **What sins did I commit?**

   _____

   _____

4. **Who needs my prayers?**

   _____

   _____

   _____

   _____

5. **What did I learn today?**

   _____

   _____

6. **What adjustments can I make in my life because of what I learned today?**

   _____

   _____

Prayers

Today is _____ S M T W TH F S

1. **What can I do to grow my relationship with God today?**
   - ☐ Read the Bible
   - ☐ Pray alone
   - ☐ Pray with a friend, family member, or spouse
   - ☐ Share my faith
   - ☐ Listen to and/or sing to Christian music
   - ☐ Write in my prayer journal
   - ☐ Serve others

2. **What can I praise and thank God for today?**

   _____
   _____
   _____
   _____
   _____

3. **What sins did I commit?**

   _____
   _____

4. **Who needs my prayers?**

   _____
   _____
   _____
   _____

5. **What did I learn today?**

   _____
   _____

6. **What adjustments can I make in my life because of what I learned today?**

   _____
   _____

Prayers

Today is _____ S M T W TH F S

1. **What can I do to grow my relationship with God today?**
   - ☐ Read the Bible
   - ☐ Pray alone
   - ☐ Pray with a friend, family member, or spouse
   - ☐ Share my faith
   - ☐ Listen to and/or sing to Christian music
   - ☐ Write in my prayer journal
   - ☐ Serve others

2. **What can I praise and thank God for today?**

   _____
   _____
   _____
   _____
   _____

3. **What sins did I commit?**

   _____
   _____

4. **Who needs my prayers?**

   _____
   _____
   _____
   _____
   _____

5. **What did I learn today?**

   _____
   _____

6. **What adjustments can I make in my life because of what I learned today?**

   _____
   _____

194

Prayers

Today is _____ S M T W TH F S

1. **What can I do to grow my relationship with God today?**
   - ☐ Read the Bible
   - ☐ Pray alone
   - ☐ Pray with a friend, family member, or spouse
   - ☐ Share my faith
   - ☐ Listen to and/or sing to Christian music
   - ☐ Write in my prayer journal
   - ☐ Serve others

2. **What can I praise and thank God for today?**

   _____
   _____
   _____
   _____
   _____

3. **What sins did I commit?**

   _____
   _____

4. **Who needs my prayers?**

   _____
   _____
   _____
   _____

5. **What did I learn today?**

   _____
   _____

6. **What adjustments can I make in my life because of what I learned today?**

   _____
   _____

Prayers

Today is _____ S M T W TH F S

1. **What can I do to grow my relationship with God today?**
   - ☐ Read the Bible
   - ☐ Pray alone
   - ☐ Pray with a friend, family member, or spouse
   - ☐ Share my faith
   - ☐ Listen to and/or sing to Christian music
   - ☐ Write in my prayer journal
   - ☐ Serve others

2. **What can I praise and thank God for today?**

   _____
   _____
   _____
   _____
   _____

3. **What sins did I commit?**

   _____
   _____

4. **Who needs my prayers?**

   _____
   _____
   _____
   _____
   _____

5. **What did I learn today?**

   _____
   _____

6. **What adjustments can I make in my life because of what I learned today?**

   _____
   _____

Prayers

Today is _____ S M T W TH F S

1. **What can I do to grow my relationship with God today?**
   - ☐ Read the Bible
   - ☐ Pray alone
   - ☐ Pray with a friend, family member, or spouse
   - ☐ Share my faith
   - ☐ Listen to and/or sing to Christian music
   - ☐ Write in my prayer journal
   - ☐ Serve others

2. **What can I praise and thank God for today?**

   _____

   _____

   _____

   _____

   _____

3. **What sins did I commit?**

   _____

   _____

4. **Who needs my prayers?**

   _____

   _____

   _____

   _____

5. **What did I learn today?**

   _____

   _____

6. **What adjustments can I make in my life because of what I learned today?**

   _____

   _____

200

Prayers

Today is _____ S M T W TH F S

1. **What can I do to grow my relationship with God today?**
   - ☐ Read the Bible
   - ☐ Pray alone
   - ☐ Pray with a friend, family member, or spouse
   - ☐ Share my faith
   - ☐ Listen to and/or sing to Christian music
   - ☐ Write in my prayer journal
   - ☐ Serve others

2. **What can I praise and thank God for today?**

   _____

   _____

   _____

   _____

   _____

3. **What sins did I commit?**

   _____

   _____

4. **Who needs my prayers?**

   _____

   _____

   _____

   _____

5. **What did I learn today?**

   _____

   _____

6. **What adjustments can I make in my life because of what I learned today?**

   _____

   _____

Prayers

Today is _____ S M T W TH F S

1. **What can I do to grow my relationship with God today?**
   - ☐ Read the Bible
   - ☐ Pray alone
   - ☐ Pray with a friend, family member, or spouse
   - ☐ Share my faith
   - ☐ Listen to and/or sing to Christian music
   - ☐ Write in my prayer journal
   - ☐ Serve others

2. **What can I praise and thank God for today?**

   _____
   _____
   _____
   _____
   _____

3. **What sins did I commit?**

   _____
   _____

4. **Who needs my prayers?**

   _____
   _____
   _____
   _____

5. **What did I learn today?**

   _____
   _____

6. **What adjustments can I make in my life because of what I learned today?**

   _____
   _____

Prayers

Today is _____ S M T W TH F S

1. **What can I do to grow my relationship with God today?**
   - ☐ Read the Bible
   - ☐ Pray alone
   - ☐ Pray with a friend, family member, or spouse
   - ☐ Share my faith
   - ☐ Listen to and/or sing to Christian music
   - ☐ Write in my prayer journal
   - ☐ Serve others

2. **What can I praise and thank God for today?**

   _____
   _____
   _____
   _____
   _____

3. **What sins did I commit?**

   _____
   _____

4. **Who needs my prayers?**

   _____
   _____
   _____
   _____
   _____

5. **What did I learn today?**

   _____
   _____

6. **What adjustments can I make in my life because of what I learned today?**

   _____
   _____

Prayers

Month in Review

What specific actions did I take toward meeting my goals?

1.
2.
3.

What did I learn this month? How did God guide me? How did God use me to bless others and to glorify Him?

_____
_____
_____
_____
_____
_____
_____
_____
_____
_____
_____
_____

What adjustments can I make in my life because of what I learned this month?

_____
_____
_____
_____
_____
_____
_____
_____
_____
_____
_____
_____
_____

Learn and pass it on: Share your personal story of how journaling strengthened your relationship with God. Fax your story to 1-800-281-6084.

Notes

Testimonials

This guide is a meaningful tool designed to
deepen a woman's relationship with God.
Susan found that journaling strengthened her
intimacy with the Lord. It is her desire
to share this resource so you, too, may grow in your faith.
It is with great pride that I bless this endeavor.
—Carol (director of Women's Ministries)

This prayer journal has really helped me get started with developing
a daily habit of prayer with God. I'm amazed at how such a simple
exercise of writing in a journal each day can have such a transforming
effect on one's life. I recommend this to anyone who is interested
in growing in their relationship with God and becoming more
discerning of His presence and guidance throughout each day.
—Helene

This workshop on prayer journaling has been so beneficial.
It has really helped me to establish the discipline of
intentionally growing in my relationship with God daily.
It's excellent for small groups!
—Jane

I bought a copy for both of my daughters. I love being
able to grow together and share what God is doing in
our lives with a simple, practical prayer journal.
—Mary

Journaling is a powerful tool for your spiritual growth.
Writing helps you fulfill the plans of the Lord.
—Jill

Writing was done thousands of years ago to teach us and provide hope. Writing gives you an opportunity to experience the greatness of God. It increases one's ability to hear the voice of God and helps us know and trust God more. As an author of multiple books, writing reveals things we would not learn on our own because prayer is two-way communication with God. Prayer involves listening to God and talking to connect to the heart of God. All my books were inspired by God via prayer and journaling. My intent is that you, too, would experience the greatness of God from praying and journaling.

—Susan A. Lund

[2]Then the LORD answered me and said: "Write the vision And make it plain on tablets, That he may run who reads it. [3]For the vision is yet for an appointed time; But at the end it will speak, and it will not lie. Though it tarries, wait for it; Because it will surely come, It will not tarry."

—Habakkuk 2:2–3 (NKJV)

Made in the USA
Monee, IL
24 September 2023